MAKING GOOD CHOICES

EVALUATING CONSEQUENCES

RACHAEL MORLOCK

PowerKiDS press™

NEW YORK

Published in 2020 by The Rosen Publishing Group, Inc.
29 East 21st Street, New York, NY 10010

Editor: Elizabeth Krajnik
Designer: Michael Flynn

Photo Credits: Cover Cavan Images/Getty Images; cover, pp. 1, 3–6, 8–10, 12, 14, 16–18, 20–24 (background) TairA/Shutterstock.com; p. 4 Andrey_Popov/Shutterstock.com; p. 5 Motortion Films/Shutterstock.com; p. 7 SpeedKingz/Shutterstock.com; p. 8 Jane0606/Shutterstock.com; p. 9 michaeljung/Shutterstock.com; p. 11 Terray Sylvester/VWPCS/AP Images; p. 12 Mike Flippo/Shutterstock.com; p. 13 Sergey Ryzhov/Shutterstock.com; p. 14 DeeaF/Shutterstock.com; p. 15 GraphicaArtis/Archive Photos/Getty Images; p. 16 Asier Romero/Shutterstock.com; p. 17 Jaren Jai Wicklund/Shutterstock.com; p. 19 Michael Zagaris/Getty Images Sport/Getty Images; p. 20 TierneyMJ/Shutterstock.com; p. 21 Veja/Shutterstock.com; p. 22 Just dance/Shutterstock.com.

Library of Congress Cataloging-in-Publication Data

Names: Morlock, Rachael, author.
Title: Making good choices : evaluating consequences / Rachael Morlock.
Description: New York : PowerKids Press, [2020] | Series: Spotlight on social
  and emotional intelligence | Includes index.
Identifiers: LCCN 2019009444| ISBN 9781725306745 (pbk.) | ISBN 9781725306776
  (library bound) | ISBN 9781725306752 (6 pack)
Subjects: LCSH: Choice (Psychology) | Decision making.
Classification: LCC BF611 .M675 2020 | DDC 153.8/3--dc23
LC record available at https://lccn.loc.gov/2019009444

Manufactured in the United States of America

CPSIA Compliance Information: Batch #CWPK20. For further information contact Rosen Publishing, New York, New York at 1-800-237-9932.

CONTENTS

CHAPTER ONE

YOU HAVE A CHOICE

Every day, you make choices that shape what you do, how you do it, and who you are. Some choices are small and can be made quickly. Other choices can have a big impact, or effect, on your health, your **relationships**, and your ability to do well in your activities. These choices can also affect the people around you. Part of making good decisions is learning how to think about these consequences.

Every day is filled with simple decisions. They're even part of the games you play. Practicing thoughtful decision-making with small choices can help you prepare for more **difficult** decisions.

Making good choices is a skill that gets better with practice. Like other skills, you can learn it by following simple steps. One important step is to evaluate, or judge, the consequences of a decision before you make it. This takes careful thought and imagination, and it can lead you to making better choices. Good decision-making is a skill you can use your whole life, whether you're at school, at home, or with friends.

CHAPTER TWO

DECISION-MAKING STEPS

Making good choices starts with a clear understanding of the problem or decision that's in front of you. Are you choosing a new after-school activity? Are you deciding when to do your homework? No matter what choice you make, your first step is to **identify** the problem.

The next step is to come up with a list of **options** to choose from. Once you know what your options are, you can evaluate them. What kind of consequences will they have? What will they affect? These questions will help you choose what to do.

Make a decision that takes the consequences of your actions into consideration. After you've made a choice, follow through on it. The final step is to look back on your decision and how it worked out. This is called reflection, and it can help you make better decisions in the **future**, too.

> Think about the last big decision you made. Maybe you chose to learn to play the trumpet in school. How did you make your choice? Did you follow any decision-making steps?

CHAPTER THREE

WHAT'S A GOOD CHOICE?

Making a good choice can be harder than you think. When you're very young, many of your decisions are simple and guided by your parents or other adults. You might choose what clothes to wear or what to eat from the options they offer you. As you get older and go to school, it's up to you to make more choices on your own. You can choose how to act at school, you can pick your friends, and you can decide what activities to join.

If you're not sure what to do, a trusted adult can help you make the best choice. They might see options or consequences that you haven't thought of on your own.

How can you tell if you've made a good choice? A good choice is one that has the greatest chance of leading to positive results. It should have the most positive outcomes not only for you, but also for everyone else **involved**. When you evaluate consequences, you compare different choices to find the one with the most likely positive results.

CHAPTER FOUR

IDENTIFYING OPTIONS

When you have to make an important decision, you might feel stuck with only one option. This is especially true if you are **stressed** or upset. You should recognize strong emotions as a signal to stop and think carefully.

Once you've slowed down your thinking, you can let your creativity kick in. Push yourself to think of other ways to solve your problem. Ask yourself questions about your decision. Think about other actions that could help you reach your goal.

In 2015, an eight-year-old boy named Levi Draheim made an unusual decision. He joined a group of other young people in a **lawsuit** against the United States. They want the government to choose better protections for the planet. Kids can select from many options if they decide to help the planet. Draheim made his choice after carefully and creatively identifying his options.

Levi Draheim's home in Florida is in danger from rising ocean water. He is the youngest of a group of 21 young people who decided to sue the United States government over **climate change**.

CHAPTER FIVE

MAKING PREDICTIONS

Once you have a list of options, you can begin evaluating them. Evaluating is all about measuring how positive or **negative** the consequences of each option could be. Since you can't try out all the options, the best way to do this is to make predictions.

A prediction is an educated guess about what will happen in the future. Predictions use your imagination, but they also rely on observations, experience, and **logic**. In addition to what you already know, you might need to find more information, or knowledge about something, to help you make a prediction.

Imagine that you're choosing to play a sport. Can you predict what might happen if you join the tennis, soccer, baseball, swimming, or basketball teams? What sports have you played before? What do you know about each team? Gathering information can help you make predictions about each option.

Before choosing a sport, find out when practices and games are, what supplies you need, and who's on the team. This can help you predict which choice will be best for you.

CHAPTER SIX

PROS AND CONS

One plan for good decision-making is to divide your predicted consequences into positive and negative sides. Benjamin Franklin wrote about this way of decision-making in 1772. A friend had sent him a letter asking for his opinion about a difficult decision. Instead of giving advice about what to choose, Franklin gave advice about how to make a choice. Franklin wrote, "My Way is, to divide half a Sheet of Paper by a Line into two Columns, writing over the one *Pro*, and over the other *Con*."

You can use Franklin's way to map out positive and negative consequences. If you have a lot of options, it might be helpful to make a different chart instead. Add a column at the beginning for each option, and line up the pros and cons related to it. Writing down ideas can help you be a more organized decision-maker.

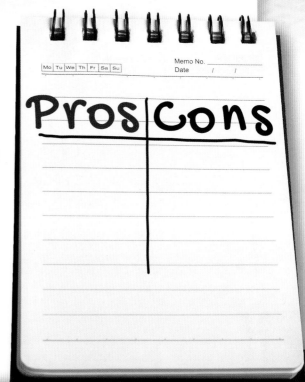

You've probably heard of lists of pros and cons before, but did you know Benjamin Franklin used them? "Pro" means "for" and "con" means "against" in Latin.

CHAPTER SEVEN

WEIGHING THE CONSEQUENCES

Franklin's advice didn't end with making the list. He also suggested comparing and balancing the two sides. The positive and negative consequences of a decision aren't necessarily equal, even if you have the same number of each. When you're evaluating your options, it's important to weigh their outcomes.

You can write out a list of pros and cons to make your ideas clearer. For quick decisions, try making a list in your head.

What are the pros and cons of going to summer camp instead of staying home? The pros might be spending time with your friends, learning to canoe, and eating dessert every night. The cons could be missing your family, feeling nervous about meeting new people, and getting bug bites. Eating dessert and getting bug bites may not be as important to you as other items on the list! Weigh each item and decide how much it matters. It could be that learning to canoe is more important to you than anything else.

CHAPTER EIGHT

VALUES AND MOTIVATIONS

The importance you place on different consequences is related to, or has to do with, your values. Your values define, or explain the meaning of, who you are as a person and who you want to be. You might value safety, kindness, fairness, doing the right thing, or fitting in with others. Those values help you decide which consequences will matter the most to you.

Sometimes, your values can **motivate** you to choose an action even if it has negative consequences. In 2016, football player Colin Kaepernick made a choice to kneel during the national anthem before football games. Usually, players stand during the anthem. Kaepernick chose to kneel to protest inequality and violence. When Kaepernick weighed the consequences of this action, he must have decided that he valued his message more than he valued fitting in with others. His actions sparked both anger and support from football fans and other fellow Americans.

What kind of consequences do you think Colin Kaepernick predicted for kneeling during the national anthem? Kaepernick lost his job but started a movement of similar protests.

CHAPTER NINE

THINKING OF OTHERS

For many people, caring for others and being kind are values that guide their actions. You should consider how a decision affects you, but you should also think about how it will affect others. Just like predicting consequences, this requires you to use your imagination. Take the perspective, or point of view, of others and try to imagine how they'll feel based on different consequences. Remember, a good decision is one that has the best outcome for everyone involved.

Thinking of you

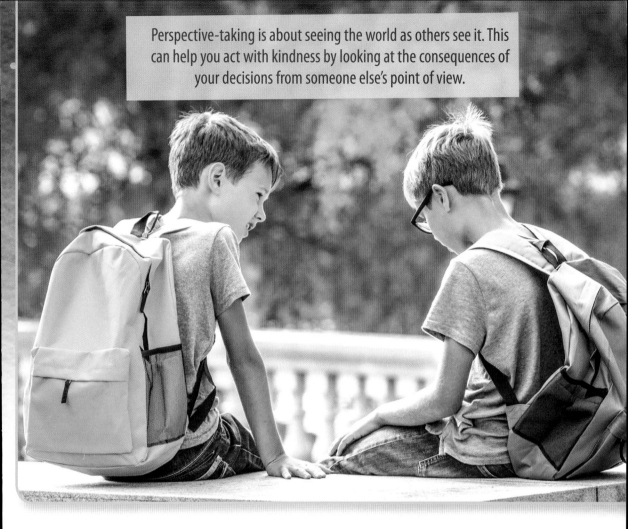

Perspective-taking is about seeing the world as others see it. This can help you act with kindness by looking at the consequences of your decisions from someone else's point of view.

What do you do if you see a classmate being bullied? If you choose not to act, there may not be any consequences for you. Now, take the perspective of your classmate. If you do nothing, they'll feel alone. If you speak up, you can help them out of a hurtful situation. Thinking about the situation from their perspective can help you make the right decision.

CHAPTER TEN

CHOOSE WISELY

Making good decisions can become a habit. It just takes practice and **critical thinking**. Pay attention to situations where you're more likely to make quick or emotional decisions. Take time to step back and think them through.

Even when you've made a thoughtful and careful decision, the results can be different than you expected. This is a good opportunity to learn. What could you do differently next time? Is there a perspective you forgot? Are some values more important to you than others? Reflecting on your past decisions can help you choose wisely in the future.

You'll be making choices every day for the rest of your life! Be sure to evaluate the consequences when you make choices that affect your health, safety, relationships, and ability to succeed. Choosing wisely can make you more independent, responsible, trustworthy, and confident.

GLOSSARY

climate change (KLY-muht CHAYNJ) Change in Earth's weather caused by human activity.

critical thinking (KRIH-tih-kuhl THING-king) Thinking that is clear and based in reason, facts, and evidence.

difficult (DIH-fih-kuhlt) Hard to do, make, or carry out.

future (FYOO-chuhr) The period of time that is to come.

identify (eye-DEHN-tuh-fy) To find out who someone is or what something is.

involve (ihn-VAHLV) To draw into a situation.

lawsuit (LAW-soot) A process by which a court of law makes a decision to end a disagreement between people or organizations.

logic (LAH-jihk) A proper or reasonable way of thinking about or understanding something.

motivate (MOH-tuh-vayt) To provide with a reason for doing something.

negative (NEH-guh-tihv) Harmful or bad. Not wanted.

option (AHP-shuhn) Something that may be chosen.

relationship (rih-LAY-shuhn-ship) A connection with someone else.

stressed (STREHSD) Feeling very worried or anxious about something.

INDEX

PRIMARY SOURCE LIST

Page 11
Levi Draheim. Photograph. Terray Sylvester. October 29, 2018. VWPCS via AP Images.

Page 15
Benjamin Franklin. Oil on canvas. David Martin. ca. 1767. Graphica Artis via Getty Images.

Page 19
Colin Kaepernick before New York Jets vs. San Francisco 49ers. Photograph. Michael Zagaris. December 11, 2016. Getty Images Sport.

WEBSITES

FEB -- 2021